BARBECUES & SALADS

Compiled by Judith Ferguson
Tested and prepared by Jacqueline Bellefontaine

1505
This edition reprinted in 1993 by Tiger Books International PLC, London
© 1987 Coombe Books
Printed and bound in Singapore
All rights reserved
ISBN 1 85501 115 8

BARBECUES & SALADS

TIGER BOOKS INTERNATIONAL
LONDON

CONTENTS

Before gas and electricity were harnessed for our cooking convenience, our ancestors employed barbecue cooking, although they didn't know it by that name. Flaming food, however, seemed to go out of fashion for a time in northern Europe, except in chafing dishes in expensive restaurants. Countries with sunnier climates kept up the art and the United States, where informality is the spirit of entertaining, adopted barbecue cooking as its own.

A barbecue grill can be a very primitive arrangement of a firebowl – a place to hold charcoal or wood – and a rack, or some support to hold the food. Modern design has added several different interpretations:

Portable barbecue grills – These are small and are often called picnic barbecues. They have folding or telescopic legs. Table-top models with short legs and hibachis in various sizes are popular styles.

Semi-portable grills – These are slightly larger and have fixed legs, sometimes with wheels for easy movement. They are often round with rotating racks, good for moving food quickly off hot-spots, or adjustable shelves. Rotisseries can be fixed to these grills and most have windshields along the back.

Hooded grills – These keep the food at an even temperature and the smoke out of the cook's eyes! With practice, whole meals can be cooked, and food can be smoked over aromatic wood chips for extra flavour.

Home-made grills – Barbecues can be built of brick or stone with oven shelves for racks.

Electric and gas grills – These use special rocks that radiate heat from electric coils or gas flames. They give the taste and appearance of charcoal-grilled food along with control over the intensity of heat. A dial with a number of settings allows more delicate foods to be cooked through without charring on the outside. These grills are cleaner and heat much faster than charcoal or wood-fired grills, which must be lit at least 1 hour before cooking. They are also nearly self-cleaning. The recipes in this book were cooked on an electric grill from Redring Electric Company.

When choosing a fuel for barbecueing, you should bear in mind that charcoal compressed into briquettes will burn for twice as long with more uniform heat than lumpwood charcoal – irregular-sized pieces of kiln-charred hardwood. However, lumpwood charcoal is easier to light than briquettes. Vine wood cuttings are an alternative to charcoal, but do not burn as long. Hardwood, such as birch or cherry can be used, but takes a long time to light and is expensive.

Firelighters, either liquid or solid, get the fire going faster. Use them to start a fire, but never, for safety reasons, on coals that are already hot. With any grill that uses charcoal or wood, be sure the fire bowl has perforations in the bottom and sides, or that the coals can sit on a perforated rack inside. This allows air to circulate underneath and makes the fire easier to light and keep going.

Special equipment is not necessary, but long-handled cooking utensils are easiest and safest to use. When grilling fish, a hinged wire rack, specially shaped for both small or large fish, is a great help. So, too, are square hinged racks for turning a number of hamburgers, sausages or steaks at the same time.

Cooking times for barbecued food cannot be very exact. There is room for variation depending on the type of grill and source of heat. For grills without adjustable shelves, results are better if the food is cooked in the oven for about half to three-quarters of the cooking time and the remaining time on the barbecue grill for colour and flavour. Similarly, larger cuts of meat, such as Butterflied Lamb, will cook faster and be juicer if pre-cooked in the oven. In fact, employ this method with any food cooked for a large group and you will avoid the problem of eating in shifts.

Salads are a natural accompaniment to barbecued food. On a warm summer's day or evening they can also be a light and refreshing meal in themselves. So when summer arrives, abandon your oven occasionally and try barbecues and salads and discover why food tastes so much better when cooked and eaten outdoors.

BARBECUES & SALADS

STARTERS / APPETIZERS AND SIDE SALADS

Satay

PREPARATION TIME: 25 minutes

COOKING TIME: 10-15 minutes

SERVES: 4 people

450g/1lb chicken, skinned, boned and cut into 2.5cm/1 inch cubes

MARINADE
30ml/2 tbsps soy sauce
30ml/2 tbsps oil
30ml/2 tbsps lime juice
5ml/1 tsp ground cumin
5ml/1 tsp turmeric
10ml/2 tsps ground coriander

SAUCE
30ml/2 tbsps oil
1 small onion, finely chopped
5ml/1 tsp chili powder
120g/4oz/1 cup peanut butter
5ml/1 tsp brown sugar
Remaining marinade

GARNISH
Lime wedges
Coriander leaves

Combine the marinade ingredients in a deep bowl. Put in the meat and stir to coat. Leave covered in the refrigerator for 1 hour. Drain and thread the meat on 4 large or 8 small skewers. Grill about 10-15 minutes, turning frequently to cook all sides. Baste often. Meanwhile heat the oil in a small saucepan. Add the onion and the chili powder. Cook until the onion is slightly softened. Take off the heat and set aside. When the meat is nearly cooked combine the marinade with the oil and onion and chili powder. Stir in the remaining sauce ingredients, thinning with water if necessary. Brush the Satay with the sauce 1 to 2 minutes before the end of cooking time. Spoon over a bit more sauce and serve the rest separately. Garnish each serving with lime wedges and coriander leaves.

This page: Rumaki (left) and Satay (right). Facing page: Grilled Garlic Prawns/Shrimp (left) aand Smoked Fish Kebabs with Horseradish Sauce (right).

Rumaki

PREPARATION TIME: 15 minutes	
COOKING TIME: 10-15 minutes	
SERVES: 4 people	

180ml/6 fl oz/¾ cup soy sauce
450g/1lb chicken livers, trimmed and cut
    into 5cm/2 inch pieces
1 200g/7oz can water chestnuts, drained
8 slices smoked streaky bacon
1 red pepper, cut in 2.5cm/1 inch pieces
Brown sugar

Combine half the soy sauce and all the chicken livers in a deep bowl. Leave to marinate in the refrigerator for 1 hour. Place the bacon slices on a wooden board. Stretch the bacon by running the back of knife backwards and forwards over each slice. Cut the slices in half across. Drain the chicken livers and discard the soy sauce. Put a piece of liver and a water chestnut on each slice of bacon and roll up. Thread on skewers, alternating with a piece of red pepper. Grill on an oiled rack above hot coals for 10-15 minutes, basting with the remaining half of the soy sauce and turning frequently. One minute before the end of cooking, sprinkle lightly with brown sugar and allow to glaze. Garnish serving dishes with parsley if desired.

Greek Salad

PREPARATION TIME: 15 minutes	
SERVES: 4 people	

1 head cos/romaine lettuce
16 black olives, stoned
120g/4oz/1 cup crumbled feta cheese
1 small can anchovies, drained
8 mild pickled peppers
60g/2oz cherry tomatoes, halved
½ cucumber, cut in small dice
30ml/2 tbsps chopped fresh oregano or
    15ml/1 tbsp dried oregano

DRESSING
120ml/4 fl oz/½ cup olive oil
45ml/3 tbsps red wine vinegar
1 clove garlic, finely minced
Salt and pepper

Wash and dry the cos/romaine lettuce and tear the leaves into bite-size pieces. Place the leaves in a large salad bowl and arrange or scatter all the other ingredients on top of the lettuce. If the anchovies are large, cut them into thinner strips or chop into small pieces. Sprinkle the fresh or dried oregano over all the ingredients in the salad bowl. Mix the dressing together well and pour over the salad just before serving.

Caesar Salad

PREPARATION TIME: 20 minutes	
COOKING TIME: 3 minutes	
SERVES: 4-6 people	

1 large or two small heads cos/romaine
    lettuce
8 slices white bread, crusts removed
120ml/4 fl oz/½ cup oil
1 clove garlic, peeled
1 small can anchovies
90g/3oz fresh Parmesan cheese

DRESSING
1 egg
120ml/4 fl oz/½ cup olive oil
Juice of 1 lemon
1 clove garlic, finely minced
Salt and pepper

Wash the lettuce and dry well. Tear the lettuce into bite-size pieces and place in a large salad bowl, or four individual bowls. Cut the slices of bread into 1.25cm/½ inch dice. Heat the vegetable oil in a small frying pan. When the oil is hot put in the clove of garlic and the cubes of bread. Lower the heat slightly and, using a metal spoon, keep stirring the cubes of bread to brown them evenly. When they are golden brown and crisp, remove them to paper towels to drain. Add the anchovies to the lettuce in the salad bowl and sprinkle on the fried bread croûtons. To prepare the dressing, place the egg in boiling water for 1 minute. Break into a small bowl and combine with remaining dressing ingredients, whisking very well. Pour the dressing over the salad and toss. Using a cheese slicer, shave off thin slices of Parmesan cheese and add to the

salad. Alternatively, grate the cheese and add to the salad with the dressing.

Smoked Fish Kebabs with Horseradish Sauce

PREPARATION TIME: 15 minutes	
COOKING TIME: 6 minutes	
SERVES: 4 people	

1 smoked kipper fillet, skinned and cut
    into 2.5cm/1 inch pieces
1 smoked haddock fillet, skinned and cut
    into 2.5cm/1 inch pieces
8 bay leaves
1 small red onion, quartered
Oil
SAUCE
30ml/2 tbsps grated fresh or bottled
    horseradish
280ml/½ pint/1 cup sour cream
10ml/2 tsps fresh dill, chopped
Salt and pepper
Squeeze of lemon juice
Pinch sugar

Thread the fish, bay leaves and slices of onion on skewers, alternating ingredients and types of fish. Brush with oil and place on an oiled grill rack above hot coals. Mix the sauce ingredients together and divide onto side plates. Grill the kebabs for about 6 minutes, turning and basting with oil frequently. When the onion is cooked, remove to serving dishes. Place kebabs on lettuce leaves, if desired, for serving.

Grilled Garlic Prawns/ Shrimp

PREPARATION TIME: 15 minutes	
COOKING TIME: 8-10 minutes	
SERVES: 4 people	

900g/2lbs uncooked king prawns/jumbo
    shrimp
60g/2oz/4 tbsps melted butter

Facing page: Greek Salad (top) and Caesar Salad (bottom).

MARINADE

3 cloves garlic, finely chopped
60ml/4 tbsps oil
120ml/4 fl oz/½ cup lemon juice
60ml/4 tbsps chopped basil
Salt
Coarsely ground black pepper

Shell and de-vein the prawns/shrimp. Leave the shell on the ends of the tails. Combine the marinade ingredients in a plastic bag. Put in the prawns/shrimp and seal the bag. Refrigerate for 1 hour, turning frequently. Place the bag in a bowl to catch possible drips. Drain the prawns/shrimp and thread onto 4 skewers. Mix the marinade with the melted butter and brush the prawns/shrimp with the mixture. Grill for 8-10 minutes about 10-15cm/4-6 inches above the coals. Brush frequently with the marinade while the prawns/shrimp cook. Pour over remaining marinade before serving.

Carrot Salad with Creamy Sesame Dressing

PREPARATION TIME: 1 hour

SERVES: 4 people

4 large carrots, peeled
120g/4oz/1 cup raisins
120g/4oz/1 cup chopped walnuts
30ml/2 tbsps sesame seeds
30ml/2 tbsps oil
15ml/1 tbsp lemon juice
90ml/6 tbsps sesame paste (tahini)
90ml/6 tbsps warm water
30ml/2 tbsps double/heavy cream
Salt and pepper
15ml/1 tbsp sugar

Place the carrots in iced water for 1 hour. Dry them and grate coarsely into a bowl. Add the raisins, nuts and sesame seeds. Mix the dressing ingredients together, adding more cream if the dressing appears too thick. If dressing separates, whisk vigorously until it comes together before adding additional cream. Toss with the carrot salad and serve.

Curried Rice Salad

PREPARATION TIME: 20 minutes

COOKING TIME: 12 minutes

SERVES: 6 people

180g/6oz/¾ cup long grain rice
15ml/1 tbsp curry powder, hot or mild as desired
4 spring/green onions, sliced
2 sticks celery, sliced
1 small green pepper, diced
10 black olives, halved and stoned
60g/2oz/¼ cup sultanas/golden raisins
60g/2oz/¼ cup toasted flaked/sliced almonds
60ml/4 tbsps flaked coconut
2 hard-boiled eggs, chopped

DRESSING
140ml/¼ pint/½ cup mayonnaise
15ml/1 tbsp mango chutney
Juice and grated rind of ½ a lime
60ml/4 tbsps natural yogurt
Salt

GARNISH
2 avocados, peeled and cut in cubes
Juice of ½ lemon or lime

Cook the rice in boiling salted water for about 12 minutes or until tender. During the last 3 minutes of cooking time drain away half the water and stir in the curry powder. Leave to continue cooking over a gentle heat until the rice is cooked and the water

This page: Carrot Salad with Creamy Sesame Dressing. Facing page: Curried Rice Salad.

is evaporated. Leave covered to stand for about 5 minutes. Toss the rice with a fork, drain away any excess water and leave to cool. Combine with the remaining salad ingredients, stirring carefully so that the hard-boiled eggs do not break up. Mix the dressing ingredients together thoroughly. Chop any large pieces of mango in the chutney finely. Stir the dressing into the salad and toss gently to coat. Arrange the rice salad in a mound on a serving dish. Sprinkle the cubed avocado with the lemon juice to keep it green and place around the rice salad before serving.

Cheese and Vine Leaves

PREPARATION TIME: 20 minutes	
COOKING TIME: 6 minutes	
SERVES: 4 people	

4 pieces goat's, feta or haloumi cheese
280ml/½ pint/1 cup olive oil
60ml/4 tbsps chopped fresh herbs such as basil, tarragon, oregano, marjoram, parsley
2 cloves garlic, peeled and crushed (optional)
1 bay leaf
Squeeze lemon juice

TO SERVE
4 fresh vine leaves, washed, or 4 brine-packed vine leaves, soaked 30 minutes
1 head radicchio
8 leaves curly endive, washed and torn in bite-size pieces

If using goat's cheese, make sure it is not too ripe. Lightly score the surface of whichever cheese is used. Mix together the oil, herbs, garlic and lemon juice. Place the cheese in a small, deep bowl or jar and pour over the oil mixture. If cheese is not completely covered, pour on more oil. Leave, covered, overnight in the refrigerator. Drain the cheese and place in a hinged wire rack. Grill the cheese over hot coals until light golden brown and just beginning to melt. Drain and dry the vine leaves. Wash the radicchio and break apart the leaves. Arrange radicchio and endive leaves on 4 small plates and

place a vine leaf on top. Place the cooked cheese on top of the vine leaf and spoon some of the oil mixutre over each serving.

Gorgonzola and Bean Salad with Pine Nuts

PREPARATION TIME: 20 minutes	
COOKING TIME: 4-5 minutes	
SERVES: 4 people	

340g/12oz French/green beans, ends trimmed
60g/2oz/½ cup pine nuts, toasted if desired
120g/4oz/1 cup crumbled gorgonzola or other blue cheese
30ml/2 tbsps red wine vinegar
90ml/6 tbsps olive oil
½ clove garlic, finely minced
Salt and pepper
2 heads radicchio

This page: Cheese and Vine Leaves. Facing page: Gorgonzola and Bean Salad with Pine Nuts (top), and Spinach Salad with Bacon, Hazelnuts and Mushrooms (bottom).

If the beans are large, cut across in half or thirds. Place in boiling salted water and cook for 4-5 minutes or until tender-crisp. Rinse under cold water and leave to drain. Toast pine nuts, if desired, at 180°C, 350°F, Gas Mark 4 for 10 minutes. Allow to cool. Mix the vinegar, oil, garlic, salt and pepper until well emulsified. Toss the beans in the dressing and add the cheese and nuts. Separate the leaves of radicchio, wash and dry. Arrange on salad plates and spoon the bean salad on top. Alternatively, tear radicchio into bite-size pieces and toss all the ingredients together.

Beetroot and Celeriac Salad

PREPARATION TIME: 25 minutes

COOKING TIME: 20 minutes

SERVES: 4 people

1 large celeriac root, peeled
4-6 cooked beets/beetroot
4 spring/green onions chopped
Juice of ½ a lemon

DRESSING
430ml/¾ pint/1½ cups sour cream
10ml/2 tsps white wine vinegar
Pinch sugar
10ml/2 tsps celery seed
25ml/1½ tbsps parsley

Cut the celeriac into 1.25cm/½ inch dice. Cook in boiling salted water with the juice of half a lemon for about 20 minutes or until tender. Drain and set aside to cool. Dice the beets/beetroot the same size as the celeriac. Mix the beets/beetroot with the spring/green onions and carefully combine with the celeriac. Mix the dressing ingredients together, reserving half of the parsley. Combine the dressing with the celeriac and the beets/beetroot, taking care not to over mix. Sprinkle the remaining parsley over the salad before serving.

Parsley Salad Vinaigrette

PREPARATION TIME: 20 minutes

COOKING TIME: 2 minutes

SERVES: 4 people

2 large bunches parsley (preferably flat Italian variety)
225g/8oz tomatoes, quartered and seeded
120g/4oz/1 cup stoned black olives, sliced
140ml/¼ pint/½ cup vegetable oil
1 clove garlic, finely minced
45ml/3 tbsps white wine vinegar
5ml/1 tsp dry mustard
Pinch sugar
Salt and pepper
60g/2oz/½ cup grated fresh Parmesan cheese

This page: Red Cabbage, Celery and Carrot Salad. Facing page: Parsley Salad Vinaigrette (top), and Beetroot and Celeriac Salad (bottom).

Pick over the parsley and discard any yellow and thick stems. Break parsley into individual leaves. Cut the tomatoes into 1.25cm/½ inch dice. Use 30ml/2 tbsps of measured oil and heat in a small frying pan. Add the finely chopped garlic and cook slowly to brown lightly. Combine with the remaining oil, vinegar, mustard, sugar, salt and pepper and beat well. Toss the dressing with the parsley, tomatoes and olives before serving. Sprinkle over the Parmesan cheese.

Red Cabbage, Celery and Carrot Salad

PREPARATION TIME: 15 minutes

SERVES: 6-8 people

1 small head red cabbage
4-6 carrots, peeled
4-6 sticks celery

DRESSING
120ml/4 fl oz/½ cup oil
15ml/1 tbsp white wine vinegar
30ml/2 tbsps lemon juice
15ml/1 tbsp honey
15ml/1 tbsp celery seed
10ml/2 tsps chopped parsley
Salt and pepper

Cut the cabbage in quarters and remove the core. Grate coarsely or

slice finely. Grate the carrots coarsely. Cut the celery into very fine strips. Combine all the vegetables in a large salad bowl or in individual bowls. Mix the salad dressing ingredients very well. This can be done by hand with wire whisk or in a blender. Once the dressing is well emulsified, add the celery seeds and whisk again. Pour over the salad and toss before serving.

Three Bean Salad

PREPARATION TIME: 15 minutes, plus marinating time

SERVES: 6-8 people

1 225g/8oz can chickpeas
1 225g/8oz can red kidney beans
1 225g/8oz can green flageolet beans
6-8 tomatoes, quartered

DRESSING
140ml/¼ pint/½ cup olive oil and
    vegetable oil mixed
60ml/4 tbsps white wine vinegar
30ml/2 tbsps chopped parsley
15ml/1 tbsp chopped basil
1 shallot, finely chopped
1 clove garlic, finely minced
Salt and pepper

Drain and rinse all the beans. Mix the dressing ingredients together thoroughly and combine with the beans. Allow to marinate for 2 hours. Mound the beans into a serving dish and surround with the quartered tomatoes to serve.

Pea, Cheese and Bacon Salad

PREPARATION TIME: 20 minutes

COOKING TIME: 15-20 minutes

SERVES: 6 people

6 strips bacon/smoked streaky bacon,
    rind and bones removed
450g/1lb fresh or frozen shelled peas
120g/4oz Red Leicester/Colby cheese
4 sticks celery, diced
4 spring/green onions, sliced thinly or
    1 small red onion, diced
1 red pepper, cored, seeded and diced

1 head Buttercrunch lettuce
180ml/6 fl oz/¾ cup sour cream or
    natural yogurt
15ml/1 tbsp chopped fresh mixed herbs
5ml/1 tsp white wine vinegar
5ml/1 tsp sugar
Salt and pepper

Dice the bacon and cook gently in a small frying pan until the fat runs. Turn up the heat and fry the bacon until brown and crisp. Remove to paper towels to drain. Meanwhile cook the peas in boiling salted water for 15-20 minutes for fresh peas and 5 minutes for frozen peas. When the peas are cooked, drain and refresh under cold water and leave to drain dry. Cut the cheese into dice slightly larger than the peas. Dice the celery and red pepper to the same size as

This page: Tomato and Mozzarella Salad with Fresh Basil. Facing page: Three Bean Salad (left), and Pea, Cheese and Bacon Salad (right).

the cheese. Combine the peas, cheese, celery, spring/green onions, red pepper and bacon in a bowl. Mix the dressing ingredients together, reserving half of the chopped mixed herbs. Combine the vegetables and bacon with half of the dressing. Separate the leaves of the lettuce and wash well. Pat dry and arrange on serving dishes. Spoon on the salad mixture and top with the remaining dressing. Sprinkle the reserved chopped herbs on top of the dressing.

Tomato and Mozzarella Salad with Fresh Basil

PREPARATION TIME: 15 minutes

SERVES: 4 people

3 large beefsteak tomatoes, sliced 6mm/
  ¼ inch thick
180g/6oz mozzarella cheese, drained,
  dried and sliced 6mm/¼ inch thick
60ml/4 tbsps coarsely chopped fresh basil
  leaves

DRESSING
90ml/6 tbsps olive oil and vegetable oil
  mixed
30ml/2 tbsps balsamic vinegar or white
  wine vinegar
1.25ml/¼ tsp Dijon mustard
Salt and pepper

GARNISH
Fresh basil leaves

Arrange the tomato slices and mozzarella cheese slices in overlapping circles on four individual salad plates. Sprinkle the fresh chopped basil leaves on top and garnish in the centre with the whole basil leaves. Mix all the dressing ingredients together very well and spoon some over the salads before serving. Serve the rest of the dressing separately.

Cracked Wheat Salad

PREPARATION TIME: 20 minutes

SERVES: 4-6 people

225g/8oz/2 cups bulgur wheat, washed
  and drained
4 spring/green onions, chopped
1 cucumber, cut in small cubes
Juice and rind of 1 lemon
4 tomatoes, cubed
4 sticks celery, diced
60g/2oz/½ cup toasted sunflower seeds
120g/4oz/1 cup crumbled feta cheese
140ml/¼ pint/½ cup olive oil
1 clove garlic, minced
Salt and pepper
60ml/4 tbsps chopped mixed herbs

Place the washed bulgur wheat in clean water and leave to soak for

5 minutes. Drain and squeeze as much moisture out as possible. Spread the wheat out onto a clean towel to drain and dry. When the wheat is dry put into a large bowl with all the remaining ingredients and toss together carefully so that the cheese does not break up. Allow the salad to chill for up to 1 hour before serving. If desired, garnish the salad with whole sprigs of herbs.

Spinach Salad with Bacon, Hazelnuts and Mushrooms

PREPARATION TIME: 20 minutes

COOKING TIME: 2-3 minutes

SERVES: 4 people

675g/1½ lbs spinach, stalks removed,
  washed and dried
6 strips bacon/smoked streaky bacon,
  bones and rind removed
225g/8oz mushrooms, sliced
120g/4oz/1 cup hazelnuts, roasted,
  skinned and roughly chopped

DRESSING
140ml/¼ pint/½ cup oil
45ml/3 tbsps white wine vinegar
5ml/1 tsp Dijon mustard
1 shallot, finely chopped
Salt and pepper
Pinch sugar (optional)

Tear the spinach leaves into bite-size pieces and put into a serving bowl. Fry or grill/broil the bacon until brown and crisp. Crumble the bacon and sprinkle over the spinach. Add the hazelnuts and mushrooms to the spinach salad and toss. Mix all the dressing ingredients very well and pour over the salad just before serving.

Cucumber and Mint Salad

PREPARATION TIME: 30 minutes

SERVES: 4 people

1 large or 2 small cucumbers, peeled for a
  striped effect or scratched with the

prongs of a fork lengthwise along the
  skin
Salt

DRESSING
280ml/½ pint/1 cup sour cream or
  natural yogurt
30ml/2 tbsps chopped fresh mint
15ml/1 tbsp chopped parsley
Pinch sugar
Squeeze lemon juice
Salt and pepper

GARNISH
Whole sprigs of mint

Slice the cucumber thinly in rounds. Place the cucumber in a colander and sprinkle lightly with salt. Leave for 30 minutes to drain. Rinse the cucumber under cold water to remove the salt and pat dry. Mix the sour cream or yogurt with the sugar, lemon juice, salt, pepper, mint and parsley. Pour over the drained cucumber and toss. Leave refrigerated for 30 minutes before serving, and garnish with whole sprigs of mint.

Potato Salad with Mustard-Chive Dressing

PREPARATION TIME: 25 minutes

COOKING TIME: 20 minutes

SERVES: 6 people

1.5kg/3lbs potatoes, new or red variety
6 sticks celery, thinly sliced
1 red pepper, seeded, cored and diced
3 hard-boiled eggs

DRESSING
280ml/½ pint/1 cup prepared
  mayonnaise
280ml/½ pint/1 cup natural yogurt
60ml/4 tbsp Dijon mustard and mild
  mustard mixed half and half
1 bunch chives, snipped
Salt and pepper

Facing page: Cucumber and Mint Salad (top), and Cracked Wheat Salad (bottom).

Cook the potatoes in their skins for about 20 minutes in salted water. When the potatoes are tender, drain and peel while still warm. Cut the potatoes into cubes and mix with the celery and red pepper. Set the potato salad aside to cool while mixing the dressing. Combine the mayonnaise, yogurt, mustard, half the chives, salt and pepper and mix well. Toss carefully with the potato salad so that the potatoes do not break up. Spoon the salad into a serving dish and slice the hard-boiled eggs into rounds, or chop roughly. Arrange the hard-boiled eggs in circles on top of the potato salad or scatter over, if chopped. Sprinkle over reserved chives and refrigerate for about 1 hour before serving.

Red, Green and Yellow Pepper Salad

PREPARATION TIME: 20 minutes

SERVES: 6 people

3 sweet red peppers
3 green peppers
3 yellow peppers
Oil
60g/2oz/½ cup small black olives, stoned
30ml/2 tbsps finely chopped coriander leaves
3 hard-boiled eggs

DRESSING
90ml/6 tbsps oil
10ml/2 tsps lemon juice
30ml/2 tbsps white wine vinegar
1 small clove garlic, finely minced
Pinch salt
Pinch cayenne pepper
Pinch sugar (optional)

Cut all the peppers in half and remove the seeds and cores. Press lightly with palm to flatten. Brush the skin side of each pepper with oil and place under a preheated grill/broiler about 15cm/6 inches from the heat. Cook until the skin chars. Remove and wrap the peppers in a clean towel. Leave them to cool 10-15 minutes. Mix the dressing ingredients and quarter the eggs. Unwrap the peppers and peel off the skin. Cut the peppers into strips about 2.5cm/

1 inch wide and arrange in a circle, alternating colours. Arrange the olives and quartered egg in the centre. Sprinkle the coriander leaves over the peppers and spoon over the dressing. Leave the salad, covered, in the refrigerator for 1 hour before serving. Peeled peppers will keep covered in oil up to 5 days in the refrigerator.

Coleslaw

PREPARATION TIME: 25 minutes

SERVES: 6 people

DRESSING
280ml/½ pint/1 cup prepared mayonnaise
4 spring/green onions finely chopped
280ml/½ pint/1 cup sour cream
60g/2oz Roquefort or blue cheese

This page: Zanzibar Prawns/Shrimp. Facing page: Coleslaw (top), and Potato Salad with Mustard-Chive Dressing (bottom).

1.25ml/¼ tsp Worcestershire sauce
5ml/1 tsp vinegar
30ml/2 tbsps chopped parsley
Pinch sugar
Salt and pepper

SALAD
1 medium size head white cabbage, shredded
6 carrots, peeled and coarsely grated
1 green pepper, cut into thin short strips
120g/4oz/1 cup roasted peanuts or raisins

Combine all the dressing ingredients, reserving half the parsley, and refrigerate in a covered bowl for about 1 hour to allow the flavours to blend. Combine the dressing with the salad ingredients and toss to serve. Sprinkle on reserved chopped parsley.

Zanzibar Prawns/Shrimp

PREPARATION TIME:	25 minutes
COOKING TIME:	18-23 minutes
SERVES:	4 people

450g/1lb king prawns/jumbo shrimp, shelled and de-veined
1 large fresh pineapple, peeled, cored and cut into chunks
Oil

SAUCE
140ml/¼ pint/½ cup orange juice
15ml/1 tbsp vinegar
15ml/1 tbsp lime juice
5ml/1 tsp dry mustard
15ml/1 tbsp brown sugar
Remaining pineapple

GARNISH
Flaked coconut
Curly endive

Thread the prawns/shrimp and pineapple pieces on skewers, alternating each ingredient. Use about 4 pineapple pieces per skewer. Place the remaining pineapple and the sauce ingredients into a food processor and purée. Pour into a small pan and cook over low heat for about 10-15 minutes to reduce slightly. Place the kebabs on a lightly oiled rack above the coals and cook about 6 minutes, basting frequently with the sauce. Sprinkle cooked kebabs with coconut and serve on endive leaves. Serve remaining sauce separately.

Egg Mayonnaise with Asparagus and Caviar

PREPARATION TIME:	25 minutes
COOKING TIME:	10 minutes
SERVES:	4-6 people

12 asparagus spears, trimmed and peeled
6 hard-boiled eggs
430ml/¾ pint/1½ cups prepared mayonnaise
15ml/1 tbsp lemon juice
Hot water
Red caviar

Tie asparagus in a bundle and cook in a deep saucepan of boiling salted water, keeping the asparagus tips out of the water. The tips will cook in the steam and the thick stalks will cook in the water, thus helping the asparagus to cook evenly. Cook about 5-8 minutes or until just tender. Rinse under cold water and

This page: Red, Green and Yellow Pepper Salad. Facing page: Egg Mayonnaise with Asparagus and Caviar.

drain. Meanwhile, place eggs in boiling water. Bring water back to the boil and cook eggs for 10 minutes. Cool completely under cold running water and peel. Combine mayonnaise and lemon juice. If very thick, add enough hot water until of coating consistency. Arrange eggs cut side down on a plate and coat with the mayonnaise. Surround with asparagus and garnish the eggs with caviar.

BARBECUES & SALADS

MEAT AND POULTRY

Kashmiri Lamb Kebabs

PREPARATION TIME: 20 minutes

COOKING TIME: 10 minutes

SERVES: 4 people

675g/1½ lbs lamb shoulder or leg
30ml/2 tbsps.oil
1 clove garlic, finely minced
15ml/1 tbsp ground cumin
5ml/1 tsp turmeric
5ml/1 tsp grated gresh ginger
Chopped fresh coriander or parsley leaves
Salt and pepper
1 red pepper, cut in 2.5cm/1 inch pieces
1 small onion, cut in rings

Cut the lamb in 2.5cm/1 inch cubes. Heat the oil and cook the garlic, cumin, turmeric and ginger for 1 minute. Add the coriander, salt and pepper. Allow to cool and then rub the spice mixture over the meat. Leave covered in the refrigerator for several hours. Thread the meat on skewers, alternating with the pepper slices. Cook about 10 minutes, turning frequently. During the last 5 minutes of cooking, thread sliced onion rings around the meat and continue cooking until the onion is cooked and slightly browned and meat has reached desired doneness.

Minced Lamb Kebabs with Olives and Tomatoes

PREPARATION TIME: 20 minutes

COOKING TIME: 10 minutes

SERVES: 4 people

30g/1oz/4 tbsps bulgur wheat, soaked and drained

550g/1¼lbs minced/ground lamb
1 clove garlic, finely minced
10ml/2 tsps ground cumin
Pinch cinnamon
Salt and pepper
1 egg, beaten
Oil
16 large green olives, stoned
16 cherry tomatoes

This page: Mustard Grilled Pork with Poppy Seeds. Facing page: Kashmiri Lamb Kebabs (left) and Minced Lamb Kebabs with Olives and Tomatoes (right).

SAUCE

280ml/½ pint/1 cup yogurt
30ml/2 tbsps chopped fresh mint
Salt and pepper

Soak the bulgur wheat until soft. Wring out and spread on paper towels to drain and dry. Mix with the remaining ingredients and enough of the beaten egg to bind together. The mixture should not be too wet. Form into small balls about 3.75cm/ 1½ inches in diameter. Thread onto skewers with the olives and tomatoes. Brush with oil and grill about 10 minutes, turning frequently. Mix the yogurt, mint, salt and pepper and serve with the kebabs.

Mustard Grilled Pork with Poppy Seeds

PREPARATION TIME: 20 minutes plus marinating time

COOKING TIME: 45 minutes to 1 hour

SERVES: 4-6 people

4 175-200g/6-7oz whole pork fillets/ tenderloin
30ml/2 tbsps black poppy seeds

MARINADE

15ml/1 tbsp mild mustard
60ml/4 tbsps oil
60ml/4 tbsps unsweetened apple juice
1 clove garlic, finely minced
Salt and pepper

SWEET MUSTARD SAUCE

280ml/½ pint/1 cup mild mustard
60g/2oz/¼ cup brown sugar
60ml/2 fl oz/¼ cup dry cider or unsweetened apple juice
10ml/2 tsps chopped fresh or crumbled dried tarragon
Pinch cayenne pepper
Salt

Mix the marinade and rub into the pork. Place the pork in a dish or pan and cover. Refrigerate for 4 hours or overnight. Using a grill with an adjustable rack, place the pork over the coals on the highest level or set an electric or gas grill to a medium temperature. Cook the pork for 45

minutes-1 hour, basting with the marinade and turning frequently. Lower the shelf or raise the temperature. Baste frequently with the sauce during the last 10 minutes of cooking time. During the last 5 minutes, sprinkle the pork fillets with the poppy seeds. Serve the pork sliced thinly with the remaining sauce.

Turkey and Pancetta Rolls

PREPARATION TIME: 30 minutes

COOKING TIME: 20-30 minutes

SERVES: 4-6 people

2 turkey breasts, 450g/1lb each, skinned
90g/3oz/⅓ cup butter softened
1 clove garlic, minced
15ml/1 tbsp oregano leaves
16 slices pancetta or prosciutto ham
Salt and pepper
Oil

Cut the turkey breasts in half, lengthwise. Place each piece between two sheets of clingfilm/plastic wrap and bat out each piece with a rolling pin or meat mallet to flatten. Mix the butter, garlic, oregano, salt and pepper together. Spread half of the mixture over each slice of turkey. Lay 4 slices of pancetta on top of each piece of turkey. Roll up, tucking in the sides and tie with fine string in 3 places. Spread the remaining butter on the outside of each roll. Cook the rolls over medium hot coals until tender. Insert a meat thermometer into each roll to check doneness. The temperature should read 90°C/ 190°F. Cooking should take approximately 20 to 30 minutes. Slice each roll into 1.25cm/½ inch rounds to serve.

Niçoise Chicken

PREPARATION TIME: 30 minutes

COOKING TIME: 20 minutes

SERVES: 4 people

4 boned chicken breasts, unskinned
60ml/4 tbsps oil
30ml/2 tbsps lemon juice

TAPENADE FILLING

450g/1lb large black olives, stoned
60ml/2 tbsps capers
1 clove garlic, peeled and roughly chopped
4 anchovy fillets
30ml/2 tbsps olive oil
Raw tomato sauce

450g/1lb ripe tomatoes, peeled, seeded and chopped
1 shallot, very finely chopped
30ml/2 tbsps chopped parsley
30ml/2 tbsps chopped basil
30ml/2 tbsps white wine vinegar
30ml/2 tbsps olive oil
15ml/1 tbsp sugar
Salt and pepper
15ml/1 tbsp tomato purée/paste (optional)

Cut a pocket in the thickest side of the chicken breasts. Combine half the olives, half the capers and the remaining ingredients for the tapenade in a blender or food processor. Work to a purée. Add the remaining olives and capers and process a few times to chop them roughly. Fill the chicken breasts with the tapenade. Chill to help filling to firm. Baste the skin side with oil and lemon juice mixed together. Cook skin side down first for 10 minutes over medium hot coals. Turn over, baste again and grill for another 10 minutes on the other side. Meanwhile, combine the sauce ingredients and mix very well. Serve with the chicken.

Orange Grilled Duck with Sesame and Spice

PREPARATION TIME: 20 minutes, plus marinating time

COOKING TIME: 40 minutes

SERVES: 4 people

4 boned duck breasts
60ml/4 tbsps sesame seeds

Facing page: Turkey and Pancetta Rolls (top) and **Niçoise Chicken** (bottom).

minutes before the duck is cooked, sprinkle the orange slices with brown sugar and grill on both sides to glaze. Serve with the duck.

Herb and Onion Grilled Lamb Chops

| **PREPARATION TIME:** 10 minutes |
| **COOKING TIME:** 15 minutes |
| **SERVES:** 4 people |

4 leg chops, cut 2cm/¾ inch thick

MARINADE
1 large onion, finely chopped
15ml/1 tbsp parsley, finely chopped
15ml/1 tbsp fresh thyme or mint leaves, roughly chopped
2 fresh bay leaves, cut in thin shreds with scissors
1 clove garlic, finely minced
45ml/3 tbsps oil
Juice of ½ lemon
Salt and pepper

Combine all the marinade ingredients and pour over the chops in a dish. Leave, covered, 2 hours in the refrigerator. Place on a rack over hot coals and cook the chops 15 minutes, turning often and basting frequently with the remaining marinade.

Barbecued Flank Steak

| **PREPARATION TIME:** 25 minutes |
| **COOKING TIME:** 45-55 minutes |
| **SERVES:** 6 people |

1.5kg/3½ lbs skirt steak/flank steak, in one piece

BARBECUE SEASONING
60ml/4 tbsps salt
7.5ml/1½ tsp freshly ground pepper
7.5ml/1½ tsp cayenne pepper (or paprika for a milder tasting mixture)

MARINADE
60ml/4 tbsps soy sauce
120ml/4 fl oz/½ cup dry white wine
45ml/3 tbsps oil
Pinch ground nutmeg
Pinch ground ginger
Pinch ground mustard
Salt and pepper

SAUCE
Reserved marinade
180ml/6 fl oz/¾ cup orange juice
1 shallot, finely chopped
10ml/2 tsps cornflour/cornstarch

GARNISH
1 orange, peeled and thinly sliced in rounds
Brown sugar

Score the fat side of each duck breast with a sharp knife. Mix the marinade ingredients together and pour over the duck in a shallow dish. Cover and refrigerate for 2 hours. Turn the duck frequently. Place the duck breasts fat side down on grill. Cook for 20 minutes per side, basting frequently. If the duck appears to be cooking too quickly, turn more often. Combine the sauce ingredients and add any remaining marinade. Cook 1 to 2 minutes over moderate heat until boiling and, just before the duck is finished cooking, brush the fat side lightly with the sauce and sprinkle on the sesame seeds. Turn fat side down onto the grill for 1 minute. Serve remaining sauce with the duck. Five

This page: Orange Grilled Duck with Sesame and Spice. Facing page: Herb and Onion Grilled Lamb Chops (top), and Barbecued Flank Steak (bottom).

Barbecued Ribs

PREPARATION TIME: 15 minutes

COOKING TIME: 2 hours

SERVES: 4-6 people

2-3 racks pork spare ribs (about 2.5kg/ 5lbs)
Barbecue Sauce (see recipe for Barbecued Flank Steak)
or
Sweet Mustard Sauce (see recipe for Mustard Grilled Pork with Poppy Seeds)

Leave the ribs in whole racks. Combine the ingredients for either sauce and pour over the meat in a roasting pan. Cover with foil and bake, turning and basting frequently, for 1 hour in a 150°C/325°F/ Gas Mark 3 oven. Uncover and bake 30 minutes more in the oven. Finish on a barbecue grill over moderately hot coals for about 30 minutes, basting frequently with the sauce. Cut between the bones into pieces. Serve with the remaining sauce.

Javanese Pork

PREPARATION TIME: 20 minutes

COOKING TIME: 30-45 minutes

SERVES: 4 people

4 pork rib or loin chops cut 2.5cm/1 inch thick
60ml/4 tbsps dark soy sauce
Large pinch cayenne pepper
45ml/3 tbsps lime or lemon juice
15ml/1 tbsp ground coriander
30ml/2 tbsps oil
30ml/2 tbsps brown sugar
4 medium-sized sweet red peppers
Oil
1 bunch fresh coriander

Snip the fat around the edges of the chops at 1.25cm/½ inch intervals to prevent curling. Mix soy sauce, cayenne pepper, lemon juice, coriander and oil together in a dish or pan. Place the pork chops in the

BARBECUE SAUCE
60ml/4 tbsps oil
340ml/12 fl oz/1¼ cups tomato ketchup
45ml/3 tbsps Worcestershire sauce
90ml/6 tbsps cider vinegar
60ml/4 tbsps soft brown sugar
60ml/4 tbsps chopped onion
1 clove garlic, crushed (optional)
1 bay leaf
60ml/4 tbsps water
10ml/2 tsps dry mustard
Dash tabasco
Salt and pepper

First prepare the barbecue sauce. Combine all the ingredients, reserving salt and pepper to add later. Cook in a heavy saucepan over low heat for 30 minutes, stirring frequently and adding more water if the sauce reduces too quickly.

Remove the bay leaf and add salt and pepper to taste before using. The sauce should be thick. Use the sauce for basting while cooking, or serve hot to accompany cooked meat and poultry. Score the meat across both sides with a large knife. Mix together the barbecue seasoning and rub 30ml/2 tbsps over the meat, reserving the rest of the seasoning for other use. Sear the meat on both sides over hot coals. Raise the grill rack or lower the temperature on a gas or electric grill/broiler. Baste with the sauce and grill the meat slowly. During last 5 minutes, lower the rack or raise the temperature and grill the meat quickly on both sides, basting with the sauce. Slice the meat thinly across the grain and serve with any remaining sauce.

This page: Javanese Pork. Facing page: Chinese Pork and Aubergine/ Eggplant Kebabs (left), and Barbecued Ribs (right).

This page: Stuffed Hamburgers. Facing page: Butterflied Lamb.

Alternatively, make shallow cuts halfway through the thickest parts and press open. Thread two or three long skewers through the meat – this will make the meat easier to handle and turn on the grill. Place in a plastic bag or large, shallow dish. Mix the other ingredients together and pour over the lamb, rubbing it in well. Cover the dish or seal the bag and leave at room temperature for 6 hours or overnight in the refrigerator. Turn the lamb frequently. Remove from the dish or the bag and reserve the marinade. Grill at least 15cm/ 6 inches away from the coals on the skin side first. Grill 20 minutes per side for pink lamb and 30-40 minutes per side for more well done lamb. Baste frequently during grilling. Remove the skewers and cut the slices across the grain. If fresh mint is unavailable, use rosemary, fresh or dried. Alternatively, roast lamb in a 180°C/350°F/Gas Mark 4 oven for half of the cooking time and grill for the last half of cooking.

Stuffed Hamburgers

PREPARATION TIME:	30 minutes
COOKING TIME:	20 minutes
SERVES:	4-8 people

900g/2lbs minced/ground beef
1 onion, finely chopped
60ml/4 tbsps Worcestershire sauce
Salt and pepper
8 hamburger buns

GUACAMOLE BURGERS

FILLING
120g/4oz Tilsit or Monterey Jack cheese, cubed
1 mild chili pepper, thinly sliced and seeds removed

TOPPING
1 avocado, peeled and mashed
1 small clove garlic, crushed
10ml/2 tsps lemon or lime juice
1 tomato, peeled, seeded and finely chopped
Salt and pepper

BLUE CHEESE BURGERS

FILLING
120g/4oz blue cheese, crumbled
30g/1oz/¼ cup chopped walnuts

marinade and leave, covered, in the refrigerator for 1 hour. Turn over after 30 minutes. Place on grill over medium hot coals or on a middle rack. Mix sugar into remaining marinade. Cook chops for 15-20 minutes on each side until well done. Baste with the marinade frequently during the last 10-15 minutes of cooking. Meanwhile, wash and dry the peppers and brush with oil on all sides. Place alongside pork for half of its cooking time. Turn the peppers often. They will soften and char on the outside. Serve the pork chops with peppers and garnish with coriander leaves.

Butterflied Lamb

PREPARATION TIME:	30 minutes, plus marinating time
COOKING TIME:	40-50 minutes
SERVES:	6-8 people

1.8kg/4lbs leg of lamb
75ml/5 tbsps oil
Juice and rind of one lemon
Small bunch mint, roughly chopped
Salt and coarsely ground black pepper
1 clove garlic, crushed

To butterfly the lamb, cut through the skin along the line of the main bone down to the bone. Cut the meat away from the bone, opening out the leg while scraping against the bone with a small, sharp knife. Take out the bone and remove excess fat. Flatten thick places by batting with a rolling pin or meat mallet.

TOPPING
15ml/1 tbsp brown/steak sauce
75ml/5 tbsps prepared mayonnaise
90ml/6 tbsps sour cream or yogurt
Salt and pepper

GRUYÈRE AND MUSHROOM BURGERS
FILLING
60g/2oz mushrooms, roughly chopped
120g/4oz Gruyère or Swiss cheese, cubed

TOPPING
450g/1lb tomatoes
1 clove garlic, finely minced
30ml/2 tbsps tarragon, chopped
15ml/1 tbsp tarragon vinegar
Pinch sugar
30ml/2 tbsps oil
Salt and pepper

Mix the hamburger ingredients well, mould the meat around the chosen fillings and press carefully into patties. Mix the guacamole topping ingredients together and set aside while grilling the hamburgers. Mix the topping for the blue cheese burgers and refrigerate until needed. For the Gruyère burger topping, roughly chop tomatoes and then finely chop in a blender or food processor. Sieve to remove the seeds and skin, combine with the remaining tomato sauce ingredients and mix well. Grill hamburgers over hot coals 10 minutes per side. Quickly grill cut sides of the hamburger buns to heat through and place the hamburgers inside. Spoon on the appropriate toppings for each filling.

Chicken Tikka

PREPARATION TIME: 20 minutes

COOKING TIME: 10-15 minutes

SERVES: 4 people

1.5kg/3lb chicken, skinned and boned

MARINADE
140ml/¼ pint/½ cup natural yogurt
1 small piece ginger, grated
1 clove garlic, finely minced
5ml/1 tsp chili powder, hot or mild
2.5ml/½ tsp ground coriander
2.5ml/½ tsp ground cumin
1.25ml/¼ tsp turmeric

1.25ml/¼ tsp red food colouring (optional)
Juice of one lime
Salt and pepper

Half head Iceberg lettuce, shredded
4 lemon wedges
4 small tomatoes, quartered

Cut chicken into 2.5cm/1 inch pieces. Mix all the marinade ingredients together. Pour over the chicken and stir well. Cover and leave for several hours in the refrigerator. Thread chicken on skewers and grill 10-15 minutes, turning frequently. Baste with any remaining marinade. Serve on a bed of shredded lettuce with tomatoes and lemon wedges.

Indian Chicken

PREPARATION TIME: 15 minutes plus marinating time

COOKING TIME: 45 minutes to 1 hour

SERVES: 4-6 people

1 1.5kg/3lbs chicken, cut into 8 pieces
570ml/1 pint/2 cups natural yogurt
10ml/2 tsps ground coriander
10ml/2 tsps paprika
5ml/1 tsp ground turmeric
Juice of 1 lime
15ml/1 tbsp honey
½ clove garlic, finely minced
1 small piece ginger, peeled and grated

Pierce the chicken all over with a fork or skewer. Combine all the remaining ingredients and spread half the mixture over the chicken, rubbing in well. Place the chicken in a shallow dish or a plastic bag and cover or tie and leave for at last 4 hours or overnight in the refrigerator. If your barbecue has adjustable shelves, place on the level furthest from the coals. Arrange the chicken skin side down and grill until lightly browned, turn over and cook again until lightly browned. Baste frequently with remaining marinade. Lower the grill for the last 15 minutes and cook, turning and basting frequently, until the chicken is brown and the skin is crisp. Alternatively, cook the chicken

in a covered pan in the oven at 150°C/325°F Gas Mark 4 for 45 minutes to 1 hour and grill for the last 15 minutes for flavour and colour. Serve any remaining yogurt mixture separately as a sauce.

Chinese Pork and Aubergine/Eggplant Kebabs

PREPARATION TIME: 20 minutes

COOKING TIME: 15-20 minutes

SERVES: 4 people

450g/1lb pork fillet/tenderloin, cut in 2.5cm/1 inch cubes
2 medium onions, cut in 2.5cm/1 inch pieces
1 large aubergine/eggplant, cut in 3.75cm/1½ inch cubes
30ml/2 tbsps Hoisin sauce
45ml/3 tbsps soy sauce
60ml/4 tbsps rice wine or dry sherry
1 clove garlic, finely minced
Sesame seeds
Salt

Sprinkle the aubergine/eggplant cubes with salt and leave in a colander to drain for 30 minutes. Rinse well and pat dry. Pre-cook in 30ml/2 tbsps oil to soften slightly. Thread the pork, onion and aubergine/eggplant on skewers, alternating the ingredients. Mix the hoisin sauce, soy sauce, rice wine or sherry and garlic together. Brush the kebabs with the mixture and place them on a lightly-oiled grill. Cook about 15-20 minutes, turning and basting frequently. During the last 2 minutes sprinkle all sides with sesame seeds and continue grilling to brown the seeds. Pour over any remaining sauce before serving.

Facing page: Indian Chicken (top), and Chicken Tikka (bottom).

Burgundy Beef Kebabs

PREPARATION TIME: 20 minutes, plus marinating time

COOKING TIME: 10 minutes

SERVES: 4 people

120g/4oz shallots or button onions, parboiled 3 minutes and peeled
670g/1½ lbs sirloin or rump steak, cut in 2.5cm/1 inch thick cubes

MARINADE
280ml/½ pint/1 cup burgundy or other dry red wine
45ml/3 tbsps oil
1 bay leaf
1 clove garlic, peeled
1 sliced onion
6 black peppercorns
1 sprig fresh thyme
Pinch salt

SAUCE
280ml/½ pint/1 cup sour cream
30g/2 tbsps chopped fresh mixed herbs (such as parsley, thyme, marjoram and chervil)
15ml/1 tbsp red wine vinegar
Pinch sugar
10ml/2 tsps Dijon mustard
Salt and pepper

Bring the marinade ingredients to the boil in a small saucepan. Remove from the heat and allow to cool completely. When cold, pour over the meat in a plastic bag. Seal the bag well, but place it in a bowl to catch any drips. Marinate overnight in the refrigerator, turning the bag occasionally. Thread the meat onto skewers with the onions and grill 10 minutes, turning and basting frequently. Mix the sauce ingredients together and serve with the kebabs.

Smoked Sausage and Apple Kebabs

PREPARATION TIME: 20 minutes

COOKING TIME: 6 minutes

SERVES: 4 people

Two rings smoked pork or beef sausage, cut in 2.5cm/1 inch thick slices

4 small apples, quartered and cored
8 sage leaves
Lemon juice
Quarter quantity sweet mustard sauce (see recipe for Mustard Grilled Pork with Poppy Seeds)

Brush the apples with lemon juice. Thread onto skewers, alternating with sausage pieces and bay leaves.

Brush with the mustard sauce and grill 10 minutes, turning frequently and basting with the sauce. Serve any remaining sauce with the kebabs if desired.

Ham and Apricot Kebabs

PREPARATION TIME: 15 minutes

COOKING TIME: 12 minutes

SERVES: 4 people

675g/1½ lbs cooked gammon/ham cut in
  5cm/2 inch cubes
225g/8oz canned or fresh apricots,
  halved and stoned
1 green pepper, cut in 5cm/2 inch pieces

APRICOT BASTE
180g/6oz/¾ cup light brown sugar
60g/4 tbsps apricot jam, sieved
90ml/6 tbsps wine or cider vinegar
5ml/1 tsp dry mustard
45ml/3 tbsps light soy sauce
Salt and pepper

Thread ham, apricots and pepper
pieces onto skewers, alternating the
ingredients. Mix the apricot baste
ingredients together and cook over
gentle heat to dissolve the sugar.
Brush over kebabs as they cook. Turn
and baste several times for about
12 minutes over hot coals. If using
canned apricots, reserve the juice and
add to any baste that remains after
the kebabs are cooked. Bring this
mixture to the boil to reduce slightly
and serve as a sauce with the kebabs.

Spicy Madeira Steaks

PREPARATION TIME: 20 minutes

COOKING TIME: 15 minutes

SERVES: 4 people

4 rump/butt steaks about 180g/6oz each

MARINADE
60ml/4 tbsps oil
140ml/¼ pint/½ cup ketchup
180ml/6 fl oz/¾ cup red wine vinegar
1 clove garlic, crushed
5ml/1 tsp pepper
5ml/1 tsp ground cloves
2.5ml/½ tsp cinnamon
2.5ml/½ tsp thyme leaves

SAUCE
140ml/¼ pint/½ cup reserved marinade
30ml/2 tbsps flour
140ml/¼ pint/½ cup beef stock
140ml/¼ pint/½ cup Madeira
Salt

Combine marinade ingredients and

pour over steaks in a dish. Cover and
refrigerate at least 4 hours. Remove
from marinade and place over hot
coals. Grill, basting frequently, until
of desired doneness. Combine flour
with reserved marinade, beating well
to mix to a smooth paste. Gradually
beat in stock. Bring to the boil in a
small saucepan, stirring constantly.
Cook until thickened, about 1

minute. Reduce heat and simmer 5
minutes. Stir in Madeira and add salt
to taste. Serve with the steak.

**Facing page: Spicy Madeira Steaks
(left), and Burgundy Beef Kebabs
(right). This page: Ham and
Apricot Kebabs (left), and Smoked
Sausage and Apple Kebabs (right).**

BARBECUES & SALADS

FISH AND SEAFOOD

Marsala Fish

| PREPARATION TIME: 25 minutes |
| COOKING TIME: 10-15 minutes |
| SERVES: 4 people |

4 medium sized mackerel, trout or similar
    fish
Juice of 1 lemon
10ml/2 tsps turmeric
2 green chili peppers, finely chopped
1 small piece ginger, grated
1 clove garlic, finely minced
Pinch ground cinnamon
Pinch ground cloves
60ml/4 tbsps oil
Salt and pepper
Fresh coriander leaves

ACCOMPANIMENT
½ cucumber, finely diced
140ml/¼ pint/½ cup thick natural yogurt
1 spring/green onion, finely chopped
Salt and pepper

Clean and gut the fish. Cut three slits
on each side of the fish. Combine
spices, lemon juice, oil, garlic and
chili peppers and spread over the fish
and inside the cuts. Place whole
sprigs of coriander inside the fish.
Brush the grill rack lightly with oil or
use a wire fish rack. Cook the fish 10-
15 minutes, turning often and basting
with any remaining mixture.
Combine the accompaniment
ingredients and serve with the fish.

Scallops, Bacon and Prawn/Shrimp Kebabs

| PREPARATION TIME: 25 minutes |
| COOKING TIME: 20-25 minutes |
| SERVES: 4 people |

12 large, raw scallops
12 raw king prawns/jumbo shrimp,
    peeled and de-veined
12 slices smoked streaky bacon/bacon
Juice of 1 lemon
60ml/2 tbsps oil
Coarsely ground black pepper

**This page: Scallops, Bacon and
Prawn/Shrimp Kebabs. Facing
page: Marsala Fish.**

RED CHILI YOGURT SAUCE
2 cloves garlic, finely chopped
1 red pepper, grilled and peeled
1 red chili pepper, chopped
3 slices bread, crusts removed, soaked in
   water
45ml/3 tbsps olive oil
140ml/¼ pint/½ cup natural yogurt

Wrap each scallop in a slice of bacon and thread onto skewers, alternating with prawns/shrimp. Mix the lemon juice, oil and pepper and brush over the shellfish as they cook. Turn frequently and cook until the bacon is lightly crisped and the scallops are just firm. Meanwhile, prepare the sauce. Squeeze the bread to remove the water and place the bread in a blender. Add the finely chopped garlic, the chopped red chili pepper and peeled red pepper and blend well. With the machine running, pour in the oil through the funnel in a thin, steady stream. Keep the machine running until the mixture is a smooth, shiny paste. Combine with the yogurt and mix well. Serve with kebabs.

Grilled Sardines with Lemon and Oregano

PREPARATION TIME: 15 minutes

COOKING TIME: 6-8 minutes

SERVES: 4-6 people

8-12 fresh sardines, gutted, scaled, washed
   and dried
8-12 sprigs fresh oregano
90ml/3 fl oz/⅓ cup olive oil
Juice and rind of 2 lemons
Salt and pepper
15ml/1 tbsp dried oregano

Place one sprig of oregano inside each fish. Mix oil, lemon juice and rind, salt and pepper together. Make two slits on each side of the fish. Brush the fish with the lemon mixture and grill over hot coals for 3-4 minutes per side, basting frequently. When the fish are nearly done, sprinkle the dried oregano on the coals. The smoke will give the fish extra flavour. May be served as a starter/appetizer or main course.

Grey Mullet with Fennel

PREPARATION TIME: 15 minutes

COOKING TIME: 18-22 minutes

SERVES: 4 people

2-4 grey mullet, depending upon size,
   gutted and cleaned

MARINADE
90ml/3 fl oz/⅓ cup oil
15ml/1 tbsp fennel seeds, slightly crushed
1 clove garlic, finely minced
Juice and rind of one lemon
30ml/2 tbsps chopped fennel tops
Salt and pepper

Heat oil and add the fennel seeds. Cook for one minute. Add the garlic and remaining ingredients except the fennel tops. Leave the mixture to cool completely. Pour over the fish in a shallow dish. Cover and refrigerate for 1 hour. Grill over hot coals 10–12 minutes per side. Sprinkle over fennel tops half way through cooking. Tops may also be placed directly on the coals for aromatic smoke.

Swordfish Steaks with Green Peppercorns and Garlic Oregano Sauce

PREPARATION TIME: 25 minutes

COOKING TIME: 15 minutes

SERVES: 4 people

30ml/2 tbsps fresh green peppercorns
   (substitute well rinsed canned green
   peppercorns)
90ml/6 tbsps lemon juice
60ml/4 tbsps olive oil
Salt
4 swordfish steaks (tuna steaks may also
   be used)

SAUCE
1 egg
1 clove garlic, roughly chopped
140ml/¼ pint/½ cup oil
15ml/1 tbsp lemon juice
2 sprigs fresh oregano
Salt and pepper

Crush the green peppercorns slightly

and mix with lemon juice, oil and salt. Place the swordfish steaks in a shallow dish and pour over the lemon oil mixture. Cover and refrigerate several hours, turning frequently. Process the egg and garlic in a blender or food processor. With the machine running, pour oil through the funnel in a thin, steady stream. When the sauce is thick, strip the leaves off the oregano and process to chop them finely. Add lemon juice, salt and pepper. Grill the swordfish over hot coals for 15 minutes, basting frequently and turning once. Serve with the sauce. (Peppercorns will pop when exposed to the heat of the grill.)

Grilled Red Mullet with Tarragon

PREPARATION TIME: 15 minutes

COOKING TIME: 10-16 minutes

SERVES: 4 people

4 large or 8 small red mullet, gutted,
   scaled, washed and dried
4 or 8 sprigs fresh tarragon

MARINADE
60ml/4 tbsps oil
30ml/2 tbsps tarragon vinegar
Salt and pepper

SAUCE
1 egg
140ml/¼ pint/½ cup oil
5ml/1 tsp Dijon mustard
15ml/1 tbsp chopped tarragon
15ml/1 tbsp chopped parsley
15ml/1 tbsp tarragon vinegar
30ml/2 tbsps double/heavy cream
5ml/1 tsp brandy
Salt and pepper

Place a sprig of tarragon inside each fish. Cut two slits on the side of each fish. Mix the marinade ingredients together, pour over the fish in a shallow dish and refrigerate for 30 minutes, covered. Put the egg in a

Facing page: Swordfish Steaks with Green Peppercorns and Garlic Oregano Sauce (top), and Grilled Sardines with Lemon and Oregano (bottom).

blender or food processor. Add the mustard, salt and pepper and process to mix. Add the oil through the funnel, with the machine running, in a thin, steady stream. When all the oil has been added, add the herbs, vinegar and brandy and process to mix well. Fold in the double/heavy cream and pour into a serving dish. Keep in the refrigerator until ready to use. Cook the fish for 5 to 8 minutes per side, depending upon size of fish. Baste frequently with the marinade while cooking. Serve with the sauce.

This page: Grey Mullet with Fennel (top), and Grilled Red Mullet with Tarragon (bottom). Facing page: Monkfish and Pepper Kebabs with Bernaise Butter Sauce.

Monkfish and Pepper Kebabs with Bernaise Butter Sauce

| **PREPARATION TIME:** 30 minutes |
| **COOKING TIME:** 25 minutes |
| **SERVES:** 4 people |

450g/1lb monkfish, cut into 5cm/2 inch pieces
8 strips bacon/streaky bacon, rind and bone removed
2 pieces lemon grass
1 green pepper, cut in 5cm/2 inch pieces
1 red pepper, cut in 5cm/2 inch pieces
12 mushroom caps
8 bay leaves
Oil

BERNAISE BUTTER SAUCE
120ml/4 fl oz/½ cup dry white wine
60ml/4 tbsps tarragon vinegar
2 shallots, finely chopped
15ml/1 tbsp chopped fresh tarragon
15ml/1 tbsp chopped fresh chervil or parsley
225g/8oz/1 cup butter, softened
Salt and pepper

Cut the bacon in half lengthwise and again in half across. Peel the lemon grass and use only the core. Cut into small pieces. Place a piece of fish on each strip of bacon and top with a piece of lemon grass. Roll up. Thread the rolls of fish on skewers, alternating with peppers, mushrooms and bay leaves. Brush with oil and grill 15 minutes, turning and basting often. While the fish cooks, heat the white wine, vinegar and shallots in a small saucepan until boiling. Cook rapidly to reduce by half. Add the herbs and lower the heat. Beat in the softened butter a bit at a time until the sauce is the thickness of hollandaise sauce. Season with salt and pepper to taste and serve with the fish kebabs.

BARBECUED VEGETABLES

Grilled Fennel

PREPARATION TIME: 15 minutes

COOKING TIME: 20 minutes

SERVES: 4 people

4 small bulbs fennel
Juice and rind of 1 lemon
60ml/4 tbsps oil
1 shallot, finely chopped
Salt and pepper

Remove the fennel tops and reserve them. Cut the fennel bulbs in half and remove the cores. Parboil the fennel for 5 minutes. Combine the juice and rind of the lemon, salt, pepper, oil and shallot. Pour over the fennel and set aside for 15 minutes. Place the fennel bulbs on hot coals and cook 15 minutes, turning often and brushing with the lemon mixture. Chop the fennel tops finely and sprinkle over the grilled fennel. Pour over any remaining lemon juice mixture to serve.

Grilled Tomatoes

PREPARATION TIME: 15 minutes

COOKING TIME: 6 minutes

SERVES: 4 people

4 beefsteak tomatoes cut in half
15ml/1 tbsp oregano, fresh or dried
30ml/2 tbsps olive oil
15ml/1 tbsp lemon juice
Salt and pepper
120g/4oz feta cheese, crumbled

Mix the oil, lemon juice, salt, pepper and oregano together. Brush over the cut side of the tomatoes and grill that side first for 3 minutes over hot coals. Brush the skin side of the tomatoes and turn them over. Grill 3 minutes more on skin side and remove the tomatoes to a serving dish. Sprinkle over the crumbled feta cheese and pour over the remaining basting mixture to serve.

Grilled Corn-on-the-Cob

PREPARATION TIME: 20 minutes

COOKING TIME: 15 minutes

SERVES: 4 people

4 large ears of corn, husks and silk
    removed, parboiled 5 minutes
120g/4oz/½ cup butter, melted
Salt and pepper
Chili powder or paprika (optional)

Brush the drained corn liberally with melted butter. Sprinkle with salt and pepper. Chili powder or paprika can be substituted for the pepper, if desired. Grill over medium hot coals for 15 minutes, turning often and basting frequently with butter. To serve, pour over any remaining butter.

Grilled Aubergine/ Eggplant

PREPARATION TIME: 30 minutes

COOKING TIME: 20-24 minutes

SERVES: 4 people

2 aubergines/eggplants
180ml/6 fl oz/¾ cup olive oil
90ml/6 tbsps lemon juice
15ml/1 tbsp cumin seed
1 clove garlic, finely chopped
30ml/2 tbsps parsley, chopped
Salt and pepper

Cut the aubergine/eggplant into rounds about 2.5cm/1 inch thick. Score the surface of each round lightly with a sharp knife, sprinkle with salt and leave to stand for 30 minutes. Heat oil for 1 minute and add the cumin seed and cook for the 30 seconds. Add the garlic and cook for a further 30 seconds. Add the lemon juice. Rinse the salt from the aubergine/eggplant slices and pat dry. Brush one side of the slices with the basting mixture. Grill on a lightly oiled rack or place in a hinged wire rack. Cook for 10-12 minutes per side until soft, basting frequently. Place the slices in a serving dish and pour over the remaining basting mixture. Sprinkle with parsley just before serving.

Grilled Mushrooms

PREPARATION TIME: 10 minutes

COOKING TIME: 15-20 minutes

SERVES: 4 people

450g/1lb large mushrooms, cleaned

MARINADE
15ml/1 tbsp chopped tarragon, fresh or
    dried
Grated rind and juice of 1 orange
15ml/1 tbsp tarragon vinegar
30ml/2 tbsps oil
Salt and pepper

Facing page: Grilled Tomatoes (top), and Grilled Fennel (bottom).

Mix together the marinade ingredients. Cut the stalks from the mushrooms and place the mushroom caps in a shallow dish. Pour over the marinade and leave the mushrooms for 15-20 minutes. Place the mushrooms in a wire rack and cook 15-20 minutes over hot coals. Brush the mushrooms frequently with the marinade and turn them once or twice. Remove to a serving dish and pour over the remaining marinade to serve.

Courgette/Zucchini, Pepper and Onion Kebabs

PREPARATION TIME:	20 minutes
COOKING TIME:	10-12 minutes
SERVES:	4 people

4-6 courgettes/zucchini, ends trimmed
1 large onion
1 large green pepper
1 large red pepper
Oil
60ml/4 tbsps dry white wine
5ml/1 tsp thyme
10ml/2 tsps chopped parsley
5ml/1 tsp chopped chives
120g/4oz/½ cup melted butter

Peel the courgettes/zucchini with swivel peeler for a striped effect. Parboil 4 minutes. Refresh under cold water. Cut in 5cm/2 inch pieces. Quarter the onion and cut in large pieces, separating the layers. Cut the peppers in half and remove the core and seeds. Cut into pieces the same size as the onion. Thread the vegetables onto skewers. Melt the butter and add the wine and cook 1 minute. Add the herbs, salt and pepper. Brush the kebabs lightly with oil and grill 5-6 minutes per side. Brush frequently with the butter mixture. When the courgettes/zucchini are tender, remove to a serving dish. Pour over the remaining butter.

Barbecued Baked Potatoes

PREPARATION TIME:	15 minutes
COOKING TIME:	25 minutes
SERVES:	4-6 people

4 large potatoes, scrubbed but not peeled
Salt and pepper
Paprika
120g/4oz/½ cup melted butter

SAUCE
280ml/½ pint/1 cup sour cream
10ml/2 tsps red wine vinegar

This page: Courgette/Zucchini, Pepper and Onion Kebabs. Facing page: Grilled Aubergine/Eggplant and Grilled Mushrooms.

5ml/1 tsp sugar
5ml/1 tsp mustard powder
5ml/1 tsp celery salt
5ml/1 tsp chopped fresh herbs

Parboil the potatoes for 10 minutes in their skins. Cut the potatoes in quarters lengthwise. Brush the potatoes with a mixture of butter, paprika, salt and pepper on all surfaces. Grill the potatoes for 15 minutes, basting frequently with the remaining butter. Meanwhile, combine all the sauce ingredients and set aside in the refrigerator until ready to serve with the potatoes.

This page: Grilled Corn-on-the-Cob (top), and Barbecued Baked Potatoes (bottom). Facing page: Hungarian Sausage Salad.

MAIN DISHES AND PASTA SALADS

Hungarian Sausage Salad

PREPARATION TIME: 25 minutes

COOKING TIME: 20-25 minutes

SERVES: 4-6 people

4 small potatoes
140ml/¼ pint/½ cup oil
45ml/3 tbsps wine vinegar
5ml/1 tsp Dijon mustard
5ml/1 tsp dill seeds, slightly crushed
15ml/1 tbsp chopped parsley
5ml/1 tsp chopped dill
Pinch hot paprika
Salt
450g/1lb sausage such as kielbasa,
    smoked pork sausage, knockwurst or
    bratwurst
1 large red onion, thinly sliced
2 green peppers, cored and sliced
4 tomatoes, quartered

Scrub and peel potatoes and cook in
salted water in a covered saucepan
for 20 minutes or until soft. Mix all
the dressing ingredients together in a
medium-sized bowl. Dice the
potatoes while still warm and coat
with the dressing. Leave the potatoes
to cool in the dressing. If using
knockwurst boil for 5 minutes. Grill/
broil the bratwurst until evenly
browned on all sides. Slice the
sausage in 2.5cm/1½ inch slices and
combine with the onion, pepper and
tomatoes. Carefully combine with
the potatoes in the dressing, taking
care not to over mix and break up
the potatoes. Pile into a large serving
dish and allow to stand for 1 hour
before serving.

Salade Niçoise

PREPARATION TIME: 20 minutes

COOKING TIME: 15-20 minutes

SERVES: 4 people

2 large potatoes, or 6 small new potatoes
180g/6oz French/green beans
4 hard-boiled eggs
1 can tuna
120g/4oz prawns/shrimp

1 can anchovies
4 ripe tomatoes
90g/3oz/¾ cup black olives, stoned
1 small cucumber, diced

DRESSING
90ml/6 tbsps olive oil
30ml/2 tbsps white wine vinegar

1 head radicchio, leaves separated and washed
1 head cos/romaine lettuce, washed
4 chicken breasts, cooked, skinned and thinly sliced
120g/4oz Bresse Bleu or other blue cheese, cut in small pieces
16 cornichons (small pickled gherkins) thinly sliced
120g/4oz cherry tomatoes, halved and cored
60g/2oz/½ cup walnut halves

DRESSING
30ml/2 tbsps vegetable and walnut oil mixed
10ml/2 tsps white wine vinegar
180ml/6 fl oz/¾ cup crème frâiche
10ml/2 tsps chopped fresh tarragon
Salt and pepper

Tear the radicchio and cos/romaine lettuce into bite-size pieces. Leave the lamb's lettuce in whole leaves. If using watercress, remove the thick stems and yellow leaves. Toss the lettuces together and pile onto a salad plate. Place the chicken, cheese, cornichons, tomatoes and walnuts on top of the lettuce. Mix the oils and vinegar together and whisk well to emulsify. Fold in the crème frâiche and add the tarragon, salt and pepper. Drizzle some of the dressing over the salad to serve and hand the rest of the dressing separately.

Pasta and Vegetables in Parmesan Dressing

PREPARATION TIME:	25 minutes
COOKING TIME:	13-15 minutes
SERVES:	6 people

450g/1lb pasta spirals or other shapes
225g/8oz assorted vegetables such as:
Courgettes/zucchini, cut in rounds or matchsticks
Broccoli, trimmed into very small flowerets

45ml/3 tbsps chopped mixed fresh herbs
10ml/2 tsps French mustard
Salt and pepper

Peel and cook the potatoes (skins may be left on new potatoes if desired) until tender. If using old potatoes, cut into 1.25cm/½ inch dice (new potatoes may be sliced into 6mm/¼ inch rounds). Trim the ends of the beans, put into boiling salted water for about 3-4 minutes or until just barely cooked. Drain and rinse under cold water, then leave to drain dry. Quarter the tomatoes, or if large cut into eighths. Quarter the hard-boiled eggs. Cut the anchovies into

short strips. Mix the dressing ingredients together and blend well. Drain oil from the tuna and mix the tuna and all the salad ingredients together. Pour over the dressing and toss carefully, so that the potatoes do not break up. Serve the salad on top of lettuce leaves if desired.

Salade Bresse

PREPARATION TIME:	20 minutes
SERVES:	4-6 people

1 bunch lamb's lettuce or watercress, washed

This page: Salade Niçoise (top), and Salade Bresse (bottom). Facing page: Pasta and Vegetables in Parmesan Dressing.

Mangetout/pea pods, ends trimmed
Carrots, cut in rounds or matchsticks
Celery, cut in matchsticks
Cucumber, cut in matchsticks
Spring/green onions, thinly shredded or
  sliced
Asparagus tips
French/green beans, sliced
Red or yellow peppers, thinly sliced

DRESSING
140ml/¼ pint/½ cup olive oil
45ml/3 tbsps lemon juice
15ml/1 tbsp sherry pepper sauce
15ml/1 tbsp chopped parsley
15ml/1 tbsp chopped basil
60g/2oz/¼ cup freshly grated Parmesan
  cheese
30ml/2 tbsps mild mustard
Salt and pepper
Pinch sugar

Cook pasta in a large saucepan of
boiling salted water with 15ml/1 tbsp
oil for 10-12 minutes or until just
tender. Rinse under hot water to
remove starch. Leave in cold water.
Place all the vegetables except the
cucumber into boiling salted water
for 3 minutes until just tender.
Rinse in cold water and leave to
drain. Mix the dressing ingredients
together very well. Drain the pasta
thoroughly and toss with the
dressing. Add the vegetables and toss
to coat. Refrigerate for up to 1 hour
before serving.

Cob Salad

PREPARATION TIME: 25 minutes

SERVES: 4-6 people

1 large head cos/romaine lettuce, washed
2 avocados, peeled and chopped
3 tomatoes, cut in small dice
1 cucumber, cut in small dice
120g/4 oz/1 cup blue cheese, crumbled
4 spring/green onions, chopped or 1 small
  red onion, chopped
120g/4 oz cooked chicken breasts, cut in
  small pieces
2 hard-boiled eggs, chopped

GREEN GODDESS DRESSING
½ can anchovies
60ml/4 tbsps chopped parsley
30ml/2 tbsps chopped basil or tarragon

30ml/2 tbsps chopped chives
Small bunch watercress, leaves only
430ml/¾ pint/1½ cups mayonnaise
15ml/1 tbsp white wine vinegar

Dry the lettuce and cut it into strips.
Tear the strips into small pieces and
put into a salad bowl. Arrange all the
ingredients on top. To prepare the
dressing, combine all the ingredients
in the blender or food processor and
purée until smooth and very green.
Serve the dressing separately with the
salad.

Crab Louis

PREPARATION TIME: 20 minutes

SERVES: 4 people

DRESSING
280ml/½ pint/1 cup mayonnaise
120ml/4 fl oz/½ cup yogurt
60ml/4 tbsps tomato chutney/chili sauce
2 spring/green onions, finely chopped
½ green pepper, finely diced
5ml/1 tsp lemon juice
Salt and pepper

450g/1lb crabmeat, flaked
1 head Buttercrunch or ½ head Iceberg
  lettuce
4 hard-boiled eggs, quartered
120g/4oz/1 cup black olives, stoned

Combine all the dressing ingredients
and mix half with the flaked
crabmeat. Arrange a bed of lettuce
on a serving dish and mound on the
crabmeat. Coat the crabmeat with
the remaining dressing. Arrange the
quartered egg and black olives
around the salad.

Julienne Salad

PREPARATION TIME: 25 minutes

SERVES: 4-6 people

1 small head Iceberg lettuce
1 small Buttercrunch lettuce
4 tomatoes, quartered
1 small red onion, chopped
½ cucumber, sliced
6 radishes, sliced
60g/2oz cooked ham
60g/2oz cooked tongue

120g/4oz cooked chicken
60g/2oz Gruyère or Swiss cheese
60g/2oz Red Leicester/Colby cheese

CREAMY HERB DRESSING
280ml/½ pint/1 cup natural yogurt
120ml/4 fl oz/½ cup double/heavy
  cream
45ml/3 tbsps fresh mixed herbs, chopped
  (use chervil, tarragon, basil, dill or
  parsley)
30ml/2 tbsps prepared mayonnaise
Salt and pepper

Tear the lettuce into bite-sized pieces
and mix with the remaining
vegetables. Divide into four salad
bowls. Slice the meats and the
cheeses into thin strips. Arrange on
top of the salad ingredients. Mix the
dressing thoroughly and serve
separately.

Lobster and Cauliflower Salad

PREPARATION TIME: 30 minutes

SERVES: 4-6 people

1 large cauliflower, washed
140ml/¼ pint/½ cup vegetable oil
45ml/3 tbsps lemon juice
5ml/1 tsp dry mustard
Salt and pepper
1 large cooked lobster
280ml/½ pint/1 cup prepared
  mayonnaise
10ml/2 tsps Dijon mustard
4 hard-boiled eggs
16 black olives, halved and stoned
2 bunches watercress, washed
Red caviar

Break the cauliflower into small
flowerets and mix with the vegetable
oil, lemon juice, mustard and salt and
pepper. Leave for at least 2 hours in a
cool place. Crack the lobster and
remove all the meat from the shell
and set aside in a small bowl. Mix the
mayonnaise and Dijon mustard. Thin
if necessary with a spoonful of hot
water. Add half the dressing to the

**Facing page: Julienne Salad (top),
and Cob Salad (bottom).**

lobster and mix carefully. Combine the cauliflower with the eggs and olives. Stir to coat the eggs with dressing but do not over-mix or break up the eggs. Remove the thick stems from the watercress and any yellow leaves. Arrange beds of watercress on four small plates. Spoon in equal portions of the cauliflower salad onto the watercress and top with an equal portion of the lobster. Coat the lobster salads with the remaining mustard mayonnaise and spoon some red caviar over the dressing.

Tuna and Pasta with Red Kidney Beans

PREPARATION TIME: 20 minutes

This page: **Tuna and Pasta with Red Kidney Beans. Facing page: Crab Louis (top), and Lobster and Cauliflower Salad (bottom).**

COOKING TIME: 10 minutes

SERVES: 4-6 people

225g/8oz/1½ cups small pasta shells
1 225g/8oz can red kidney beans,
*   drained and rinsed*

120g/4oz small mushrooms, quartered
1 can tuna, drained and flaked
4 spring/green onions, sliced
30ml/2 tbsps chopped mixed herbs

DRESSING
140ml/¼ pint/½ cup olive oil
45ml/3 tbsps white wine vinegar
Squeeze lemon juice
15ml/1 tbsp Dijon mustard
Salt and pepper

Cook the pasta shells in boiling salted water with 15ml/1 tbsp oil for 10 minutes or until just tender. Rinse under hot water and then place in cold water until ready to use. Mix the dressing ingredients together thoroughly and drain the pasta shells. Mix the pasta with the beans, mushrooms, tuna, spring/green onions and chopped mixed herbs. Pour over the dressing and toss to coat. Chill up to 1 hour in the refrigerator before serving.

Mariner's Salad

PREPARATION TIME: 25 minutes

COOKING TIME: 15 minutes

SERVES: 6 people

450g/1lb pasta shells, plain and spinach
4 large scallops, cleaned
280ml/½ pint/1 cup frozen mussels, defrosted
140ml/¼ pint/½ cup lemon juice and water mixed
120g/4oz shelled and de-veined prawns/ shrimp
140ml/¼ pint/½ cup cockles or small clams, cooked
4 crab sticks, cut in small pieces
4 spring/green onions, chopped
15ml/1 tbsp chopped parsley

DRESSING
Grated rind and juice of ½ lemon
280ml/½ pint/1 cup mayonnaise
10ml/2 tsps paprika
90ml/3 fl oz/⅓ cup sour cream or natural yogurt
Salt and pepper

Cook the pasta for 10 minutes in a large pan of boiling salted water with 15ml/1 tbsp oil. Drain and rinse under hot water. Leave in cold water

until ready to use. Cook the scallops and mussels in the lemon juice and water mixture for about 5 minutes or until fairly firm. Cut the scallops into 2 or 3 pieces, depending upon size. Mix the dressing and drain the pasta thoroughly. Mix all ingredients together to coat completely with dressing. Stir carefully so that the shellfish do not break-up. Chill for up to 1 hour before serving.

Italian Pasta Salad

PREPARATION TIME: 25 minutes

COOKING TIME: 10 minutes

SERVES: 4-6 people

450g/1lb pasta shapes
225g/8oz assorted Italian meats, cut in strips: salami, mortadella, prosciutto, coppa, bresaola
120g/4oz provolone or fontina cheese, cut in strips
15 black olives, halved and stoned
60g/4 tbsp small capers
120g/4oz peas
1 small red onion or 2 shallots, chopped
160g/6oz oyster mushrooms, stems trimmed and sliced

DRESSING
45ml/3 tbsps white wine vinegar
140ml/¼ pint/½ cup olive oil
½ clove garlic, minced
5ml/1 tsp fennel seed, crushed
15ml/1 tbsp chopped parsley
15ml/1 tbsp chopped basil
15ml/1 tbsp mustard
Salt and pepper

Cook the pasta in a large saucepan of boiling water with a pinch of salt and 15ml/1 tbsp oil. Cook for about 10 minutes or until just tender. Add the frozen peas during the last 3 minutes of cooking time. Drain the pasta and peas and rinse under hot water. Leave in cold water until ready to use. Mix the dressing ingredients together well and drain the pasta and peas thoroughly. Mix the pasta and peas with the Italian meats and cheeses, olives, capers, chopped onion or shallot and sliced mushrooms. Pour the dressing over the salad and toss all the ingredients together to coat. Do not over-mix.

Leave the salad to chill for up to 1 hour before serving.

Shrimp and Cashews in Pineapples with Tarragon Dressing

PREPARATION TIME: 30 minutes

COOKING TIME: 10 minutes

SERVES: 4 people

2 small fresh pineapples
225g/8oz small cooked shrimp
120g/4oz/1 cup roasted unsalted cashew nuts
2 sticks celery, thinly sliced
60ml/4 tbsps lemon juice

DRESSING
1 egg
30ml/2 tbsps sugar
15ml/1 tbsp tarragon vinegar
120ml/4 fl oz/¼ pint whipping cream
10ml/2 tsps chopped fresh tarragon or 5ml/1 tsp dried tarragon, crumbled

Cut the pineapples carefully in half lengthwise, leaving the green tops attached. Carefully cut out the flesh and remove the cores. Cut the flesh into bite-size pieces. Combine the shrimp, cashews and celery and toss with the lemon juice. Spoon the mixture into the pineapple shells and refrigerate to chill. To prepare the dressing, beat the egg and sugar together until light in a heat-proof bowl. Add the vinegar and tarragon, place the bowl over hot water. Whip with a wire whisk until thick. Take off the heat and allow to cool, whisking occasionally. When cold, lightly whip the cream and fold into the dressing. Spoon over the salad and serve in the pineapple shells.

Facing page: Italian Pasta Salad (top), and Mariner's Salad (bottom).

Oriental Salad

PREPARATION TIME: 25 minutes

COOKING TIME: 2 minutes

SERVES: 4-6 people

1 cake tofu, cut in small cubes
140ml/¼ pint/½ cup vegetable oil
120g/4oz mangetout/pea pods, ends
  trimmed
60g/2oz mushrooms, sliced
60g/2oz broccoli flowerets
2 carrots, peeled and thinly sliced
4 spring/green onions thinly sliced
2 sticks celery, thinly sliced
60g/2oz/½ cup unsalted roasted peanuts

120g/4oz bean sprouts
½ head Chinese leaves/cabbage, shredded

DRESSING
45ml/3 tbsps lemon juice
10ml/2 tsps honey
5ml/1 tsp grated ginger
45ml/3 tbsps soy sauce
Dash sesame oil

Drain tofu well and press gently to remove excess moisture. Cut into 1.25cm/½ inch cubes. Heat 30ml/2 tbsps from the 140ml/¼ pint/½ cup oil in the wok or frying pan. Save the remaining oil for the dressing. Cook the mangetout/pea

This page: Oriental Salad. Facing page: Shrimps and Cashews in Pineapple with Tarragon Dressing.

pods, mushrooms, broccoli, carrots and celery for 2 minutes. Remove the vegetables and set them aside to cool. When cool mix them together with the onions, peanuts and bean sprouts. Mix the dressing and pour over the vegetables. Add the tofu and toss carefully. Arrange a bed of Chinese leaves/cabbage on a serving dish and pile the salad ingredients on top to serve.

SALADS WITH FRUIT

Waldorf Salad

PREPARATION TIME: 20 minutes

SERVES: 6 people

4 sticks celery, diced
4 apples, mixture of red-skinned and
green-skinned, diced
180g/6oz grapes, black and white, halved
and seeded
120g/4oz/1 cup walnuts or pecans,
roughly chopped
280ml/½ pint/1 cup prepared
mayonnaise
60ml/4 tbsps heavy cream
Juice of half a lemon

Mix the celery, apples, grapes and nuts together and toss with the lemon juice. Lightly whip the cream; fold into the mayonnaise. Fold the dressing into the salad and serve chilled. If desired, substitute raisins for the grapes and garnish with 30ml/2 tbsps chopped parsley.

Fruit Salad with Coconut Cream Dressing

PREPARATION TIME: 30 minutes

SERVES: 6-8 people

900g/2lb fresh assorted fruit, such as:
Pineapple, peeled, cored and cut in
wedges
Melon, skinned and sliced
Bananas, peeled, cut in thick rounds and
sprinkled with lemon juice
Apricots, halved and stoned and sprinkled
with lemon juice
Peaches, peeled and sliced and sprinkled
with lemon juice
Strawberries, hulled and washed
Raspberries or blackberries washed

Papaya, peeled and sliced
Currants, stems removed
Blueberries/bilberries, washed
Kiwi, peeled and sliced
Kumquats, thinly sliced, seeds removed
Fresh figs, quartered
Pears, peeled, cored and sliced

DRESSING
280ml/½ pint/1 cup natural yogurt
140ml/¼ pint/½ cup coconut cream
30-45ml/2-3 tbsps lime juice
Seeds of 1 fresh pomegranate

Arrange assortment of fruit on plates. Mix together the ingredients for the dressing and drizzle over the fruit. Sprinkle on the pomegranate seeds.

Green and Gold Sunflower Salad

PREPARATION TIME: 15 minutes

SERVES: 4 people

2 large ripe avocados
8 ripe apricots

DRESSING
45ml/3 tbsps sunflower oil
15ml/1 tbsp lemon juice
Salt and pepper

YOGURT DRESSING
140ml/¼ pint/½ cup natural yogurt
10ml/2 tsps honey
Grated rind of 1 lemon
10ml/2 tsps chopped parsley
60g/4 tbsps toasted sunflower seeds
1 small Buttercrunch lettuce, washed and
separated into leaves

Prepare the oil and lemon juice dressing. Cut avocados in half and remove the stones. Peel and cut into slices. Cut apricots in half and

remove the stones. If the apricots are large cut in half again. Add the apricots to the avocados, spooning over the dressing. Mix all the ingredients for the yogurt dressing together except the sunflower seeds. Place the lettuce leaves on salad plates and arrange the avocado and apricots on top. Spoon over some of the yogurt dressing and sprinkle the sunflower seeds onto the dressing. Serve immediately and hand extra dressing separately.

Watercress and Orange Salad

PREPARATION TIME: 20 minutes

SERVES: 4-6 people

3 large bunches watercress, well washed
and thick stalks removed
4 oranges, peeled and segmented

DRESSING
90ml/6 tbsps vegetable oil
Juice and rind of 1 orange
Pinch sugar
Squeeze lemon juice
Salt and pepper

Break watercress into small sprigs and discard any yellow leaves. Arrange the watercress with the orange segments on plates or toss in one large salad bowl. Mix the dressing ingredients together very well and pour over the salad just before serving.

Facing page: Watercress and Orange Salad (top), and Waldorf Salad (bottom).

Fennel, Orange and Tomato Salad

PREPARATION TIME: 25 minutes

COOKING TIME: 3-4 minutes

SERVES: 4 people

2 bulbs fennel, green top trimmed and
*   reserved*
2 large, ripe tomatoes
2 oranges

DRESSING
30ml/2 tbsps orange juice
25ml/1½ tbsps lemon juice
Zest of 1 orange
90ml/3 fl oz/⅓ cup olive oil and
*   vegetable oil mixed half and half*
5ml/1 tsp chopped fresh oregano or basil
Pinch sugar
Salt and pepper

Choose fennel with a lot of feathery green top. Reserve the tops. Cut the cores out of the bottom of the fennel bulbs and discard. Bring water to the boil in a large saucepan. Slice the fennel thinly, lengthwise, and place the slices in the boiling water. Cook until becoming translucent and slightly softened, about 3-4 minutes. Carefully remove the slices to a colander and rinse under cold water. Leave to drain. Place the tomatoes into the boiling water for 5-10 seconds. Put immediately into cold water. Peel and slice into 6mm/ ¼ inch rounds. Grate or use a zester to remove the peel from 1 orange.

This page: Fruit Salad with Coconut Cream Dressing. Facing page: Green and Gold Sunflower Salad (top), and Fennel, Orange and Tomato Salad (bottom).

Peel off the pith with knife and peel the remaining orange. Slice both oranges into 6mm/¼ inch rounds. Prepare the dressing by whisking all the ingredients very well and reserving the orange zest. Arrange the fennel, tomato and orange slices in circles on a round serving dish. Pour over the dressing and sprinkle on the orange zest. Chop the fennel tops and sprinkle over or use whole to garnish the salad.

INDEX